Original title:
The Roof of Comfort

Copyright © 2025 Creative Arts Management OÜ
All rights reserved.

Author: Arabella Whitmore
ISBN HARDBACK: 978-1-80587-150-7
ISBN PAPERBACK: 978-1-80587-620-5

Sails of Solace

A ship of cushions floats in air,
With snacks and pillows everywhere.
The captain's hat, a jester's crown,
We sail to places upside down.

The sails are blankets, warm and bright,
We steer through dreams by starry light.
The waves are giggles, soft and fun,
We ride them all till day is done.

A Nest for the Weary

In branches high, a cozy space,
Where tired souls can find their place.
Birds play tag, both loud and quick,
While squirrels practice acrobatic tricks.

The eggs are cushions, warm and round,
Cracking jokes, the laughter sounds.
A feathery blanket, snug and tight,
In this nest, all's well tonight.

Refuge of the Soul

A tent of laughter welcomes all,
With rubber chickens on the wall.
Inside the glow of giddy glee,
We hide from life and feel so free.

The floor is made of marshmallow dreams,
We bounce around, or so it seems.
With every joke and silly face,
We find our bliss in this strange place.

The Guardian's Embrace

An oversized teddy guards the light,
With chocolate bars tucked out of sight.
His arms are wide, a silly grin,
Inside his hug, we let love in.

He whispers tales of silly lore,
While tickling toes and asking for more.
This giant friend, in fluff so true,
Brings joy and comfort, just for you.

Clouded Comfort

In a house with pillows soft and wide,
Lies a cat that thinks it's got great pride.
It sprawls out like a king on a throne,
While I squeeze in like I'm carved from stone.

The fridge is stocked with snacks galore,
I nibble and munch, then I nibble some more.
My couch is a vessel of chips and cheese,
It's where I reside, with the greatest of ease.

Outside it rains, but I don't care,
In my fuzzy slippers, I twirl in the air.
The cat looks bemused as I dance with glee,
I might just do this for eternity!

So here's to the days of comfort and fun,
Where lounging and laughing are just never done.
With snacks in abundance and a cat on my lap,
I've found my own roof in this heavenly nap.

Sheltering Whispers

Under a tree, with squirrels so spry,
I shared my sandwich, the bread went dry.
A birdy squawked, it wanted a bite,
Turns out it's the world's first feathered knight!

Rain tapped gently as giggles flowed,
With puddles forming, a splashy road.
Umbrella upside down, my hat took flight,
Who knew wet socks could bring such delight!

Under the Canopy of Solace

In a hammock strung between two trees,
I heard the bees buzz, and oh, what a tease!
A breeze tickled leaves, like nature's laugh,
While ants marched proudly, led by their staff.

A branch gave way and I did a spin,
Plopped on the ground, now that's the win!
Up in the branches, my snacks took flight,
The laughter of squirrels? Well, that's an invite!

When Shadows Embrace

In the shade of a hat, I lounged with grace,
While shadows danced, just keeping pace.
A lizard winked, oh so sly and cool,
I asked, "Join me for a dip in the pool!"

But lizards don't swim; they stick to the rocks,
I splashed around, annoying the cocks.
With each splash made, the chickens took flight,
Turns out they wanted to end their night!

Haven Above the Storm

Underneath this huge, old eave,
Raindrops dance while I cleverly weave.
Caught in my thoughts, a thought got stuck,
A wet sock party? Best of luck!

As thunder rumbled, the cat made a leap,
Landed on my lap—oh, what a heap!
We both looked at each other, eyes wide as moons,
Amidst the storm's roar, we hummed happy tunes!

Warmth of Celestial Embrace

Under the blanket of night, quite vast,
Where the stars do twinkle and dance so fast.
I grab a cocoa, take a silly sip,
And spill it on my chin—a hilarious trip!

The moon grins wide with a cheeky light,
Making shadows that giggle, oh what a sight!
I trip on my cat, in my fluffy sock,
A clumsy ballet, I'm the star of the block!

Hearth of Tranquil Nights

The fireplace crackles, like popcorn it pops,
While I fumble with marshmallows, my aim surely flops.
One lands in my drink, making it bubbly,
I laugh as my friends watch, their faces turn rubbery!

With blankets like capes, we're heroes tonight,
Sipping hot chocolate, not a care in sight.
But the fire's a tease and sparks fly in the air,
We dodge them like ninjas, with a comical flair!

Canopy of Serenity

Beneath a tree's branches, a hammock does sway,
I try to get in, but flip the wrong way!
Sailing through space with a squeak and a shout,
I land in the grass, and laughter's the route!

The leaves whisper secrets, they giggle and sigh,
As I bounce up again, a butterfly flies by.
With snacks strewn around like a feast in the sun,
I munch and I wiggle, oh what silly fun!

The Sanctuary of Gathering Stars

On a rooftop picnic, we gather with glee,
But ants think my sandwich is theirs, oh me!
With a squeal and a run, I protect my dear lunch,
Like a warrior in battle, I leap with a crunch!

The stars are our audience, twinkling at night,
As we tell goofy tales, everything feels right.
One friend starts to snore, the others all stare,
A symphony of snores, to the moon we declare!

Embracing the Night Sky

Stars beget a canvas bright,
Where crickets chirp and sing with delight.
A squirrel's dance on the fence so fine,
Who knew for mischief, they'd dare to climb?

Moonlit shadows play tricks and tease,
The cat's sneaky pounce does not aim to please.
Giggling ghosts in pajamas waltz,
Socks on their ears, oh what a vault!

Where Dreams Find Refuge

In a hammock strung between two trees,
A raccoon whispers his nightly tease.
Dreams fly by like a kite aloft,
While owls hoot at the squirrels who scoff.

Pillows piled high like mushroom clouds,
Laughter erupts from the hidden crowds.
Slippers chase shadows on a silly spree,
Under this shelter, we're all so free!

The Arch of Tenderness

A rainbow arches over our heads,
As we sip our tea on giant beds.
Bunnies bounce in their fuzzy suits,
In search of lost, mismatched boots.

Lollipops grow like flowers in spring,
And every sneeze brings a confetti fling.
With giggles echoing, we embrace the cheer,
This is the magic that lingers near!

Guardians of Gentle Slumber

Pillow forts guard the realm of rest,
Where dreams go wild, and giggles are best.
A dragon snores in the corner tight,
While unicorns join the midnight flight.

Lullabies hum from a toaster's glow,
As gummy bears dance in a soft fuego.
In this kingdom of silliness and peace,
Every wacky moment will never cease!

Homeward Bound Under Starlight

The cat shimmies down the hall,
While dog is waging war with the ball.
A sofa springs appear to play,
As snacks fly by in disarray.

The fridge hums tunes of midnight snacks,
While socks conspire in overt attacks.
The remote's lost, the chaos reigns,
Yet, laughter echoes through the lanes.

Shelter from Shadows

The dust bunnies dance a jig and twirl,
While sweaters cling like a superhero's curl.
Cushions serve as anything but seats,
A fortress built from crumbs and sweets.

The light flickers with a cheeky flare,
As shadows argue in the tiny air.
Yet, within this chaos, joy is found,
In laughter's echo, we are unbound.

Embrace of Serenity

Worn-out chairs creak with delight,
As pillows hold whispers through the night.
A teacup sings the tales of sips,
While the kettle joins in jovial quips.

The blanket fort gains royal fame,
As the TV claims the crown of game.
From tangled cords and joyful screams,
Home whispers comfort in our dreams.

Sanctuary Above the Turmoil

Wild socks dance on the floor's parade,
While the clock ticks loud, and plans cascade.
A picture frame tips and gives a cheer,
As memories rise like bubbles of beer.

The window cracks a smile with the moon,
While crickets play their late-night tune.
In hidden corners, the giggles sprout,
In this sanctuary where love's about.

Beneath a Blanket of Peace

In a den where snacks abound,
A couch that swallows, round and round.
We fight for space, both cat and pup,
In this vast sea, we cozy up.

The TV's on, yet we don't care,
A pillow fight fills the fragrant air.
With laughter loud and silly dreams,
This blissful chaos bursts at seams.

A warm embrace, so full of cheer,
We huddle close, no room for fear.
With fuzzies here and tickles there,
A laugh parade beyond compare.

So here we stay, in funny bliss,
A blanket fort, a playful kiss.
Our hearts are light, our spirits free,
In this hilarious family spree.

Echoes in a Cozy Nest

Nestled snug, like peas in a pod,
We drift in dreams, a cozy facade.
Echoes of giggles chase the gloom,
As popcorn pops in the living room.

With mismatched socks on every chair,
And cats that leap without a care.
Our home's a tale of silly lore,
Where every stumble opens doors.

A dance-off starts, we twist and twirl,
As merchandise flies—oh, such a whirl!
Amidst the chaos, love shines bright,
In every jest, there's pure delight.

So here we thrive, with hearts aglow,
In the realm we make, our joys bestow.
With laughter echoing in the night,
We find our peace in this delight.

Where Love Lingers

In corners where the snacks reside,
We playfully argue who will decide.
With each sweet bite, our joy expands,
As Jellybean fights for our hands.

The pet parade rolls through the hall,
With furballs bouncing, they never stall.
Each gentle pounce is met with glee,
In this love-laced comedy spree.

We reminisce about silly times,
When spilled milk became comic crimes.
Each chuckle bubbles through the room,
Creating light where once was gloom.

So here we sit, with hearts so grand,
In a love-filled home that understands.
Where laughter lingers, tucked away,
In silly bliss, we frolic and sway.

Soothing Shadows of Home

With shadows dancing on the floor,
A memory strikes, and then there's more.
The couch becomes our royal throne,
Where all our quirks have brightly shone.

As tacos fall and cheese takes flight,
We laugh and share with sheer delight.
A crazy mix of silly charms,
This joyful place, with open arms.

We battle for the blanket's claim,
With every giggle, we stake our fame.
As pillows fly and toes get tugged,
In this safe haven, we feel snugged.

So let the shadows softly fall,
Our silly stories, we recall.
Within these walls, our hearts do roam,
In soothing echoes, we find home.

Perch of Hope

On the peak where birds forget,
They dance with dreams, no room for fret.
A squirrel juggles acorns with glee,
While clouds tiptoe, just wait and see.

With tea on hand, the lantern glows,
As laughter spills like summer prose.
A raccoon wears a top hat so bright,
Inviting all to join the delight.

The breeze hums tunes of silly cheer,
Whispers tales only we can hear.
And on this perch, we find our peace,
Where worries tumble, laughter won't cease.

So raise a toast to the joy we find,
Under skies where worries unwind.
Silly shenanigans rule the day,
In our lofty lair, we laugh and play.

Arcadian Hideaway

In a nook where giggles bloom,
And sunbeams dance in every room.
A cat in shades takes a sunbath,
While frogs perform their silly math.

With cookies stacked, a teapot sings,
Gossamer webs weave funny things.
A duck in a bowtie struts around,
While mismatched socks lay on the ground.

Jokes hang like fruit in the air,
And laughter spins in every chair.
In this slice of whimsical dreams,
Life is sweeter than it seems.

So come, let's play beneath this sky,
Where even clouds can burst and cry.
Humor wraps us in its delight,
In our hideaway, all feels right.

Cloistered Dreams

Within these walls, a mischief brews,
A cactus dons a pair of shoes.
The ceiling fans hum songs of mirth,
In this sanctuary of carefree birth.

A parrot cracks jokes from its perch,
While shadows dance in a playful lurch.
With pillows flying all around,
Silly antics in leaps abound.

The clock ticks backwards, don't be shy,
As butterflies walk on by and sigh.
Here, the world's a circus of glee,
And every moment's a jubilee.

So let craziness take the stage,
In the theater of a happy age.
Where dreams giggle and come to life,
In cloistered corners, free from strife.

Encircled by Ease

In a grove where humor thrives,
A doughnut tree high-fives the hives.
Sunshine sprinkles through the leaves,
Where drones of humor weave and cleave.

A fairy juggles among the spry,
As a snail races by with a pie.
The flowers chuckle, gossip loud,
In this easy realm, we're all proud.

With marshmallow clouds to float and fly,
And ice cream rivers running by.
Every corner bursts with a grin,
As good cheer dances under the skin.

So gather 'round this merry spree,
Let laughter echo, wild and free.
In this embrace of breezy fun,
Life's better when we play as one.

Under the Dome of Affection

Beneath a sheltering wink,
Laughter dances, drinks a drink.
Cupped in warmth, like sweet hot stew,
We giggle, share absurdity too.

Whenever skies decide to frown,
We swap our frowns for laughter's crown.
With pillows tossed, we strike a pose,
Rolling with jokes, like old-time pros.

The cat may plot a feline coup,
But here we laugh while sipping brew.
Jokes fly high like kites in spring,
In this cocoon where giggles cling.

So let the clouds throw their worst pitch,
For in this nook, we find our niche.
Together, we'll spin whimsical tales,
Spinning happiness, like wind in sails.

Haven of Restful Hearts

In beanbag hills, we lie and scheme,
Plotting dreams like a comic meme.
Socks mismatched, hair in a swirl,
Chasing the oddities of the world.

A family of fluff and squeaks,
We share our snacks, and sneak some peaks.
An empire of crumbs, joyful mess,
Turning simple moments into a fest.

The room is a circus, laughter rings,
While a rubber chicken wildly swings.
Under blankets piled, we safe-keep,
Our giggles echo, we barely sleep.

So here we lounge, hearts intertwined,
In silliness and joy, we unwind.
A goofy tale at every turn,
In this safe space, bright lessons learned.

Lanterns in the Twilight

As daylight fades, our lanterns glow,
Racing shadows like a sleepy show.
We crack silly jokes, a laughter spree,
In the twilight's warmth, as free as can be.

A smudge of chocolate on my nose,
My friends all tease, the laughter grows.
With cookies crumbled, tales unwind,
In this twinkle-lit realm, joy is blind.

Cuddle close in quirky attire,
A dance of silliness we conspire.
The breeze chuckles with a gentle tease,
As we share dreams like dandelion seeds.

Forgotten worries, tucked away tight,
In this glow, everything feels right.
Together in whimsy, our spirits take flight,
As lanterns flicker, we shine through the night.

Comfort Found in Stillness

In the silence, where randomness reigns,
We lounge about, avoiding our strains.
Bingeing on laughter and half-baked schemes,
Creating comfort from silly dreams.

With mismatched pajamas and wild bedhead,
The world outside can stay uninspired.
Pillow fights ensue with goofy glee,
Turning our haven to a circus spree.

Tea bags dance in cups with flair,
While arguing who sat in that chair.
Time stands still as the echoes swell,
In this fortress where all's laughable well.

So let the world rush, spin and dash,
We'll make our moments forever last.
For in the stillness, our hearts play part,
Finding comfort in the joy we impart.

Under the Cloak of Night

Beneath the stars, we hide from fright,
A raccoon steals my snack, what a sight!
With cookies falling, we laugh so loud,
In shadows dancing, we're just so proud.

The moon grins down, quite the jest,
A cat joins in, thinking it's best.
It pounces on shadows, leaps like a clown,
As I'm stuck searching for my missing crown.

A searchlight shines, the neighbors frown,
While we're giggling, losing our gown.
The night's our stage, chaos anew,
What a funny debut, just me and you.

So here we sit, under the sky,
With mischievous grins, oh me, oh my!
In laughter's embrace, we revel in bliss,
We'll remember this night, we'll surely miss!

Whispers of Contentment

In cozy corners, we nestle tight,
With books piled high, what a delight!
A cup of cocoa, complete with foam,
The perfect recipe to feel at home.

Socks mismatched but hearts aligned,
Laughter echoes, it's well-designed.
Pajamas on, we shimmy and sway,
Dancing clumsily in a silly display.

The cat joins in, pulling a stunt,
Knocking down yarn, what a fun hunt!
With gentle chuckles, the hours fly,
Under laughter's charm, we no longer shy.

In whispered dreams, our spirits soar,
With every giggle, we yearn for more.
Tomorrow's chaos will have to wait,
For now, let's cherish this perfect state!

The Embrace Beyond the Horizon

On sandy shores, we build a nest,
With seashells for pillows, we find our zest.
A seagull swoops, trying to tease,
And steals our chips with the greatest ease.

A funny dance by the rolling tide,
We trip and tumble with nothing to hide.
Sand in our hair, and laughter in air,
Nothing is serious; we haven't a care.

With waves that crash as the sun dips low,
We pretend to surf, what a wild show!
Each splash a riot, each tumble a cheer,
In our laughter, we conquer the fear.

As twilight whispers, the sky alight,
With colors that twinkle, oh what a sight!
We'll craft memories like grains in the sand,
In giggles, we find our joy so grand.

Serenity's Silent Song

In a garden bright, the flowers sway,
With bees that buzz in their own ballet.
A squirrel scampers, its frantic race,
Tripping over petals, a funny face.

Beneath the shade, we pause to snack,
With chips and laughter filling the pack.
A butterfly flutters, trying to tease,
And lands right in my drink, oh geez!

We play a game of 'who can sit still',
As laughter erupts, it's such a thrill.
Silence is golden, but not tonight,
With giggles breaking the tranquil night.

So here we lounge, sweet peace our theme,
With jokes and pranks, we plot and dream.
In quiet moments wrapped in glee,
Serenity dances, just you and me!

Veil of Tranquility

Beneath the quilt of lazy hues,
Socks dance like they're in the blues,
A cat sprawls wide, a royal throne,
While snacks perform their crunching tone.

Pillows sing sweet lullabies,
While snacks are always in disguise,
Remote's lost, we search in vain,
As popcorn pops in rhythmic strain.

Chasing dreams on a wild ride,
In fuzzy slippers we abide,
With ice cream cones that melt away,
Life's a party, come what may.

Under blankets, we conspire,
To dance as if we had a choir,
With laughter bubbling, hearts so light,
Each moment's pure unfiltered delight.

Refuge of the Heart

In a fortress made of couch and throw,
Where every laugh has room to grow,
We sip our coffee, spill the tea,
As chaos swirls, we simply flee.

The walls are lined with playful dreams,
As silly jokes burst at the seams,
Each pillow fight a fierce ballet,
In giggles, worries drift away.

Card games turned to wild bets,
As we gamble on our fates and pets,
A mini dance in fuzzy socks,
We dodge the chores like crafty fox.

With crumbs as stardust on our faces,
We reign supreme in comfy places,
Every snort and snicker shared,
In this kingdom, no heart's ensnared.

Nurtured Above the Winds

Nestled high on fluff clouds we see,
A land where all snacks are free,
Tangled up in jumbled sheets,
We laugh until our heart just beats.

Sipping smoothies, feeling grand,
With each blunder, we take a stand,
A toast to mishaps, spilled drinks too,
In joyful chaos, we push through.

Daring dreams of sky-high fun,
In mismatched socks, our numbers run,
A fort of pillows and giggling glee,
With laughter echoing endlessly.

As the winds whisper outside our gate,
Inside, we craft our silly fate,
In this haven of mirth and cheer,
Every moment feels sincere.

Calm Under the Cosmos

Beneath the stars, our laughter twirls,
As gummy bears dance, and joy unfurls,
With moonlight casting goofy grins,
We chase the night as mischief spins.

Blankets form a wobbly den,
Where every laugh brings light again,
A cosmos filled with playful schemes,
In this dream, we map our dreams.

With each tickle fight, we soar,
Caught in giggles, we beg for more,
Astronauts lost in silly space,
In our universe, we find our place.

As stardust glitters in the night,
We toast to jokes in pure delight,
In synchrony, our hearts take flight,
Wrapped in comfort, all feels right.

Settee of Warmth

In the corner, sits a chair,
It creaks and squeaks, yet doesn't care.
With cushions plump, it's quite the sight,
You melt right in, and feel just right.

The cat sprawls wide, takes up the space,
With fur so soft, it wins the race.
You sip your tea, pretend to read,
While all around, the world does speed.

Your snack's a mess, crumbs here and there,
But in this spot, you've not a care.
The world outside can do its worst,
In this embrace, you'll quench your thirst.

So grab a novel, or take a nap,
This cozy spot is quite the trap.
Just watch out for that sudden sneeze,
Or you might wake and feel the breeze.

Spirit's Shelter

Beneath a roof of chocolate dreams,
Where laughter's echo always beams.
The walls are lined with silly quotes,
And floor's a game of toss-the-coats.

On rainy days, we form a train,
To hug the pillows once again.
With comfort snacks stacked in a pile,
We laugh and roll, and do it in style.

The dog comes by to steal a bite,
His wagging tail's a comical sight.
With family jokes that never cease,
This spirit's den, it's pure release.

So here's to chortles, and all that's bright,
In this haven, we feel just right.
When life's a mess, come take a seat,
Where every moment feels so sweet.

Shroud of Serenity

In realms where chaos can't intrude,
A blanket's warmth, oh what a mood.
Wrapped up tight, like a little burrito,
With dreams of pizza, oh so completo.

My slippers squeak like ducks on stride,
They wiggle 'round, I glide with pride.
With popcorn flying to the ceiling,
This cozy corner's got that feeling.

The world out there, a comic show,
But here I lounge, with no need to go.
My pants are tight, I made my choice,
In this blanket fort, I rejoice.

So let life whirl and dance about,
In my cocoon, I have no doubt.
With hugs of fabric and snack so near,
This silly shelter brings me cheer.

Arc of Restfulness

Like a rainbow after rain's delight,
This quirky nook feels just right.
A hammock swings with glee and flair,
I close my eyes, do not a care.

The snacks are hid in secret spots,
Behind the books and used-up pots.
As nature calls, I hold it back,
And treat this space like loyal Jack.

With old guitars to strum a tune,
And quotes that make me laugh so soon.
In this small space, the world's at bay,
A happy funk, come what may.

So float away on fluffy dreams,
In silly socks and mismatched themes.
Forget your worries, let them flee,
This arc of joy's our jubilee.

An Arch of Gentle Secrets

Beneath the arch, we giggle low,
Whispers dance, like breezes flow.
Curious squirrels join the chat,
Sharing tales of the neighborhood cat.

Every secret, a shade of cheer,
Even the ones that disappear.
We laugh at clouds that try to peek,
And wear our smiles, quite unique.

In this spot, life is a jest,
Where worries dwindle, find some rest.
Jokes bounce like balls up in the air,
Sprinkling joy, we've plenty to share.

With each chuckle, we find our place,
In this arch, a warm embrace.
Life's humor keeps us feeling light,
Together here, everything's right.

Umbrella of Emotions

An umbrella bright, with colors galore,
Saves us from feelings we often ignore.
We dance in the rain, splashes on the ground,
Making puddles of laughter, joy all around.

Shadows shiver under our playful sway,
While we laugh at the clouds that lead us astray.
A gust blows by, a hat takes flight,
We chase after it, what a silly sight!

Emotions swish like the whirling breeze,
We sing out loud, we do as we please.
With every droplet, a giggle grows,
Under this umbrella, see how love flows?

In the storm's heart, we find our song,
A kaleidoscope of feelings, all day long.
We twirl and spin 'til the sun breaks through,
With an umbrella of laughter, we're never blue.

Perch of Stillness

On a branch, we rest, like birds in glee,
Watching the world, just you and me.
The squirrels juggle acorns, one by one,
While we ponder what's truly fun.

In moments of calm, we giggle bright,
As leaves rustle softly, taking flight.
Nature's quiet, a gentle tease,
A whispering wind, one that aims to please.

Here, we find peace in the playful sound,
Of chirping crickets that leap around.
Every tickle of breeze on our skin,
Reminds us where laughter truly begins.

So let's stay perched, with sighs of bliss,
In this stillness, we won't miss.
For in our hearts, fun takes its place,
A sweet, easy rhythm, our favorite space.

Aerial Embrace

In the hug of the sky, we float so free,
Clouds become pillows, just you and me.
We spin and twirl, on dreams so high,
With laughter like bubbles that fill up the sky.

Each gust a nudge, propelling our glee,
As sunbeams paint rainbows for us to see.
The world below seems small and shy,
While we soar above, letting worries fly.

A dance of eagles, a flip of a kite,
Cracking jokes in the soft sunset light.
With every dip, we can't help but grin,
In this aerial realm, let the fun begin!

So let's spread our arms on this wind-swept race,
With giggles that echo through open space.
For in this embrace, we find our tune,
Rolling with laughter, under the moon.

Abode of Repose

In the corner, there's a chair,
With snacks piled high, beyond compare.
A cat sits judging from on high,
While I just munch and watch the sky.

The table wobbles, what a sight,
Each thud's a dance, oh what delight.
The remote's lost, what's on today?
My couch's calling, come what may!

Socks on the floor like little foes,
Surprises found in every pose.
I hunt for peace, it eludes me here,
But giggles dance, and that's quite clear.

So come and join this messy spree,
In this abode, just you and me.
With laughter bright and crumbs to spare,
We'll conquer chaos without care.

Shielding Embrace

A blanket fort that's built so high,
With fairy lights to light the sky.
Crackers crunch as secrets spill,
And soda pops, what a thrill!

My pets convene, their council grand,
To guard my snacks, they take a stand.
A cheese slice falls, the frenzy starts,
This fortress holds the bravest hearts.

A pillow fight, a gentle shove,
We laugh, we tease, we push and shove.
The walls might sag, but spirits soar,
In this embrace, who could want more?

So here we huddle, all tucked in,
With laughter echoing, thick and thin.
The world outside can clutch its woes,
We are the kings, just look at those!

Purlieu of Peace

The porch swing creaks in rhythmic bliss,
With lemonade served, who could resist?
Under a sun that shines so bright,
We dream of nothing, just pure delight.

Mosquitoes buzz, but we don't care,
With sandy toes and messy hair.
The grill's ablaze, oh what a feast,
While bees dance 'round, a lively beast.

The gardener's hat is quite a sight,
In flowered shorts, he roams at night.
He talks to plants, they're in a trance,
We chuckle softly at their dance.

So linger here, let troubles fade,
In this purlieu, memories made.
A sunny smile, a silly jest,
In this sweet spot, we feel so blessed.

Sanctuary of the Soul

In my nook, where ideas bloom,
The socks are lurking, quite the gloom.
A cup of tea spills, what a mess,
Yet here I conjure my happiness.

The bookshelf leans with tales untold,
While dust bunnies dance, brave and bold.
The world outside can pound and sway,
Inside this space, I'll laugh and play.

A jigsaw puzzle, a cat's warm lap,
With giggles stifled, and dreams on tap.
Mark my words, this joy won't cease,
In corners tight, I find my peace.

So take a seat, let's share a laugh,
In this sanctuary, don't you dare half.
We'll banter while time walks away,
In silly moments, we'll forever stay.

Elysian Nook

In a corner of the room, a cat takes a nap,
Dreaming of fish, and plotting a trap.
The cushions are soft, the snacks are divine,
Who knew comfort could also involve wine?

Laughter erupts in a bubble of cheer,
With every mishap, we hold our breath near.
A spill of the drink, a jump of the pup,
In this warm sanctuary, we all raise our cup.

The clock ticks away, but we've lost track of time,
As we dance to the tunes of our own silly rhyme.
A slip on the rug, and down goes Aunt May,
With giggles and gasps, we help her up, hey!

Under this roof, where the silly resides,
We gather like bees, in our dreams we confide.
With camaraderie shared, and jokes that we sing,
This nook is a place where joy's always king.

Canopy of Compassion

Beneath a big blanket, we huddle and smile,
In a fortress of laughter, we stay for a while.
Hot cocoa spills over, but we don't care much,
For the warmth of our chatter is the sweetest touch.

The dog steals a cookie, it's a sight to behold,
As we groan and we grin, it's part of the mold.
With giggles and snorts, we weave tales of the past,
In this funny haven, good times are amassed.

A game of charades, oh, what a delight,
We stumble and fumble, but spirits are bright.
The cat, unimpressed, watches from the chair,
With a look that says, "You all are quite rare."

In this canopy wide, we find joy anew,
Each moment a treasure, in our goofy crew.
With love wrapped around, like a warm fuzzy sweater,
Nothing can dampen our giggles, not ever!

Serene Vista

Through windows wide open, the breezes do flow,
As we share our wild stories, letting laughter grow.
The plants are all smiling, joined in our jest,
Even they know that absurd is the best.

On the couch, we lounge with snacks piled high,
A chip on the floor, who knows how it flew by?
With pillows as shields, we engage in our jokes,
"Duck!" Is a shout that brings all the folks.

Oh, the remote is lost, and the channel's a haze,
As we search and we scrounge in a most hilarious craze.
With popcorn in hand, we can't keep a straight face,
In this realm of comfort, we've found our place.

The sunsets are magic, but laughter's the key,
With a wink and a nudge, we let silly be free.
From dusk until dawn, with our hearts all aglow,
In this vibrant oasis, our silly sides grow.

Quietude's Alcove

In a nook full of cushions, we gather for fun,
With games and with giggles, our hearts weigh a ton.
The couch makes us giddy, so cozy and wide,
It's a carnival ride with your best friend by your side.

The lamp's casting shadows, we create a parade,
A dance of the silly, while old songs serenade.
With a slip and a trip, oh what a scene,
As we tumble and wriggle, it feels like a dream.

On the table, a feast fit for kings and queens,
Beneath all the chaos, flow delicious cuisines.
A cake made of spinach? Oh, what a display!
We eat those odd choices and laugh all the way.

In this alcove so quiet, our hearts leap and soar,
With giggles that echo, we always ask for more.
Though time may fly fast, in these charming embrace,
We'll savor each tick, in this hilarious space.

Nook of Nurturing

In a corner of the room, wide and bright,
Cats dance with socks, what a funny sight!
Laundry piles high, a mountain we climb,
Yet laughter echoes, it's silliness time.

Cookies baking, oh what a sweet smell,
But one just dropped, it fell like a shell!
With giggles and crumbs all over the floor,
We laugh as we sniff, who can ask for more?

Children giggle, a ruckus they make,
Tripping on toys, oh what a mistake!
Yet in this chaos, joy is the prize,
Laughter erupts, and the heart simply flies.

Gathered close, under blankets we squeeze,
Sharing our stories, as sweet as you please.
In this cozy nook, we find our delight,
Wrapped up in love, everything feels right.

Asylum of Affection

In a kitchen bustling, pots clang and chime,
Mom jokes about cooking, a laugh every time!
With flour on faces, and dough on the floor,
We create our mess, but we laugh even more.

Dad trips on the rug, a twist and a spin,
He asks for a hug, we chuckle and grin.
With hearts full of warmth, and pies on the rack,
This haven of humor never lacks a knack.

Grandpa tells tales, of when he was small,
Bouncing on beds, oh he had a ball!
With laughter erupting, what fun it all seems,
In our joyful haven, reality beams.

Silly moments blossom, like flowers in spring,
This asylum wraps us, with joy on a string.
For here, every chuckle, every tear we share,
Builds bridges of love, strong enough to bear.

Overarching Calm

Under a wide sky, with kites that take flight,
We run with the breeze, what a wonderful sight!
Dogs chase the wind, with a bark and a leap,
In this expansive space, we find laughs to keep.

Sipping on lemonade, as the sun starts to set,
We toast to the day, it's the best one yet!
Stories are traded, with giggles we share,
Each tale a reminder, of love in the air.

Trees sway like dancers, a funny old show,
Whispering secrets, to those down below.
We tumble and roll, like leaves in a storm,
In this playful realm, we feel safe and warm.

As night softly falls, and the stars blink above,
We gather together, in silence and love.
With laughs in our hearts, and peace on our minds,
This overarching calm, is what joy really finds.

Celestial Refuge

When the sky is a canvas, with colors so bold,
The clouds wear big hats, like stories retold.
We giggle at rainbows, so vivid and bright,
In this celestial space, everything feels right.

Moonbeams are laughing, in silver-white gowns,
While stars play their games, as they tumble down.
We build our own castles, in the soft gleam of night,
With whispers and wishes, our dreams begin flight.

The comets do waltzes, as we dance on the ground,
While Mars joins the party, spinning around.
With laughter that echoes, and joy that won't fade,
This heavenly hideout is vastly arrayed.

In our cozy retreat, as the nighttime unfolds,
We share all our secrets, and stories untold.
With a wink from the stars, and a chuckle from space,
Our refuge of giggles, holds a warm, sweet embrace.

Haven of Harmony

In this snug nook, where socks do pair,
The cat plays king, without a care.
Pillows piled high, a mountain grand,
Where laughter echoes, oh so unplanned.

Cupcakes on the table, scattered like dreams,
And mismatched mugs, bursting at the seams.
Here's a space for giggles, not for sorrow,
Join the fun, there's always tomorrow.

Gadgetry rampant, with a twist of fate,
A blender spins tales that just can't wait.
The telly's on, but no one can see,
We're dancing like fools, wild and free.

With play-dough walls and crayon skies,
A place where nonsense merrily flies.
This home's a circus, come take a seat,
Where joy is the tune, and life's a sweet treat.

Harbor of Healing

In the corner, a chair is sagging low,
A blanket fortress, where we let dreams flow.
Cookies and cream, the snacks divine,
Where laughter's the remedy—better than wine.

Old stories linger like dust in the air,
Each giggle a wave, softens every care.
Friends gather round with wild tales to share,
A toast to the moments when life feels rare.

The cat, our mascot, prowls with great pride,
A fluffy dictator, no need to hide.
Pasta conquests, a true Italian feast,
Don't ask the chef—he's too fond of yeast.

In the night's embrace, the lights twinkle bright,
We dance with our shadows, dodging the fright.
In this haven built by laughter and cheer,
We find our patch, we hold it near.

Tranquil Dome

Under the arch, a cozy retreat,
With mismatched chairs that wobble on feet.
Bubble baths swirl with scents that entice,
Where laughter erupts and spices the slice.

A ceiling painted with stars made of yarn,
Hiding our secrets, never to barn.
The quirks of our crew lend charm like a song,
With socks on our hands, we sing all night long.

Never a dull day, monotony's foe,
With pillows as shields, we counter the woe.
A dance with a broom sends worries away,
In our dome of delight, we play and we sway.

Here, cupcakes rain like confetti from dreams,
While sitcoms play out in ridiculous themes.
We lift our spirits with joyful repartee,
In our tranquil dome, come join and be free!

Sweet Shielding

Beneath the eaves, where shadows conspire,
Laughter ignites like a wild campfire.
Sugar-filled stories spill through the cracks,
Each moment a treasure, a number of snacks.

The fish bowl bubbles, and the dog wears a pout,
Each corner's a canvas where joy's painted out.
With blankets like clouds, we float through the night,
Relishing nonsense until the sunlight.

Here, the tea's steeping, the manners take flight,
Banter as sweet as a slice of delight.
With silly reflections in puppy dog eyes,
We build castles of friendship that never capsize.

So pull up a chair; let your worries all melt,
In this quirky retreat, love and laughter are felt.
Our silly shenanigans, a safe, warm embrace,
Come join the fun; there's always more space.

Cradle of Comfort

In the corner, a cat takes a nap,
A blanket tucked, creating a trap.
With a snore that could wake the whole block,
She dreams of chasing her favorite sock.

Mismatched socks, they lay in a heap,
A testament to the chaos we keep.
And as the laundry tumbles and spins,
I sip my coffee while chaos wins.

A spill on the table, a dance of surprise,
The dog rushes in, oh how he flies!
In the mess, laughter erupts like a fountain,
These moments of joy make me feel mountainous.

With every corner, there's laughter anew,
My silly old home, warm and askew.
Each quirk a reminder of love that is free,
In this cradle of comfort, it's just you and me.

Enclosed in Stillness

In the quiet, my fish takes a swim,
I watch as he glides with whimsical whim.
A bubble escapes, rising to greet,
He looks like a king on a throne, what a feat!

The clock ticks away with a rhythm so sly,
Each tick is a giggle, oh my oh my!
With every chime, my knees start to shake,
If only these walls would rattle and quake!

The shadows dance, making shapes on the floor,
A creature has formed, I can't take it anymore!
I swear it just winked; it's pulling my leg,
Some days I think I'm losing my peg!

But in this stillness where silliness reigns,
I find my own laughter despite all the strains.
Enclosed in these walls where my heart finds its thrill,
Life's little quirks give me all the goodwill.

Overhanging Tranquility

Beneath the shades of the old mango tree,
Sits a squirrel plotting his next jamboree.
He looks at the world with such grand intent,
Planning his feast, oh what a content!

A breeze carries giggles from neighboring yards,
As our lawn chairs unfold, we lower our guards.
With lemonade splashes, the air's filled with cheer,
Each sip a reminder of moments so dear.

The cats play tag, oh what a sight,
They tumble and roll, such furry delight!
With feathers and strings as their chosen toys,
Their antics create such wonderful noise.

Though everything's simple, laughter spills bright,
In this odd little nook, our spirits take flight.
Overhanging tranquility, branches that sway,
This joy from the chaos colors our day.

Dome of Delight

Under the glow of the kitchen's warm light,
A dance-off erupts, what a hilarious sight!
With spatulas waving, we bust out our moves,
Each twist and twirl, oh how the laughter grooves!

A pie in the oven, the aroma's divine,
But who knew the dog thought it was all fine?
With a cheeky grin and a leap to the table,
He snatches a slice, thinking he's able!

A tap on my shoulder, my friend's lost in glee,
With flour on noses, we're as happy can be.
And through all the chaos, not a frown in sight,
Just laughter and love wrapped in moonlight.

In this dome of delight, let the fun never cease,
Where silliness lives and we find our peace.
With cupcakes and dreams, and friendships so bright,
Every little moment feels perfectly right.

Eave of Dreams

Beneath a hat of stars so bright,
I dream of snacks in the moonlight.
A raccoon steals my chips with glee,
I shout, 'Hey buddy, leave some for me!'

On cloudy days, I dodge the rain,
With umbrella tricks, I'm quite the bane.
I dance around with grace, not much,
Until I trip and shout, 'Not the crutch!'

A parrot squawks, it's quite the scene,
Stealing my jokes, he's a real mean machine.
I laugh so hard, I spill my tea,
He looks at me like, 'What's wrong with thee?'

In the eave's embrace, we play all day,
With laughter echoing, come what may.
I ponder if dreams can sometimes be,
Just silly wishes, like going sky-free!

Nest of Peace

In a cozy nook where fluffballs meet,
Birds chirp tales about snacks that are sweet.
They plot to steal my last donut,
But when they see me, they laugh and run.

A cat named Whiskers, always so sly,
Stretches and yawns, and gives it a try.
He dreams of a world with no pesky mice,
But ends up on a skateboard, oh what a slice!

I sip my cocoa, it's raining outside,
While squirrels conduct their nutty joyride.
They scamper and chatter, their fun's on repeat,
While I sit back, caught up in the beat.

With pillows stacked high like a fortress of fluff,
The nest gives me shelter, but I'm still not tough.
In this haven of giggles, I close my eyes tight,
And dream of the day I can fly like a kite!

A Shield of Solace

With quirky hats that wobble and sway,
I wear my laughter like a sunny bouquet.
The clouds rumble jokes, not thunder, you see,
While raindrops giggle, 'Come dance with me!'

Beneath my shield, the woes fade away,
As clouds form the shapes of cats at play.
I toss my worries like confetti in air,
And laugh as the world spins without a care.

The sun pops out, a grinning surprise,
While squirrels conspire with mischief in their eyes.
They throw acorns like they're planning a game,
While I join the antics; oh, what a fame!

In this wacky refuge, I burst with delight,
My heart's a balloon that floats to new heights.
A shield made of chuckles and whimsical dreams,
Where life is a skit with silly extremes!

Corral of Calmness

In a corral of giggles, we gather each day,
Where llamas wear hats in a comical way.
I sit and giggle as they prance around,
They trip on their tails and tumble down to the ground.

A cow with a bowtie juggles some hay,
While roosters strut like they own the day.
I laugh till I'm weak, with tears in my eyes,
As farm life becomes a show of surprise.

My trusty old dog plays an old guitar,
Singing 'How to Cook Like a Celeb Star!'
The barn fills with echoes of barking delight,
As we dance with the shadows, till the fall of night.

In this corral, we ride the winds of cheer,
With every belly laugh, I hold my friends near.
With comfort in humor, we let worries flee,
As I muse, 'Life is best with a hint of silly!'

A Canopy of Calm

Under a blanket of popcorn nights,
Laughter hangs like twinkling lights.
Squirrels debate in high-pitched tones,
As I sip tea and chat with stones.

Pillows declare a soft rebellion,
While my dog dreams of a million felons.
With each hiccup, joy takes flight,
Inside this cozy, silly delight.

Chasing the cat as it leaps and bounds,
We weave tales of craziness profound.
Here, the world's worries fade away,
While gnomes plot mischief in broad daylight.

My socks squeak tales of socks so bold,
While my slippers seek warmth from the cold.
A serenade of giggles posh,
Under this roof, my heart's a squash.

Haven Beneath the Stars

Nighttime blankets dance and twirl,
As fireflies do their twinkling whirl.
Crickets snap their fingers so loud,
To wake up the moon and please the crowd.

Under this dome of mismatch dreams,
Where marshmallows float in caramel streams.
A raccoon steals my sandwich, oh dear!
Yet laughter erupts instead of a tear.

Galaxies wobble with each silly quip,
While owls hoot tunes that make us flip.
Stars buzz gossip, oh what a scene,
As I sip cocoa from my green cuisine.

Tales of yore with a twist or two,
As the sun begins to peek through.
But there's no rush to end the spree,
In this haven, we are forever free.

Refuge in the Rain

Raindrops tap on the window pane,
While ducks in hats parade through the lane.
Umbrellas boogie and spin about,
In this downpour, there's no room for doubt.

Clouds grumble like an old man's fuss,
Yet puddles challenge things to jump and rush.
I splash and shudder, my socks all wet,
But giggles echo, a joyful duet.

A cat in boots sells tea with grace,
As umbrellas turn into a fanciful race.
How silly to worry about a dreary day,
When laughter pours in a thrilling display.

The rain might pour, but inside it's fun,
Each drop a dance under lights like the sun.
So let the clouds grumble and churn,
For in this refuge, we laugh and learn.

Hearth of Whispers

In the corner, tales of warmth unfold,
Where socks and shoes share secrets bold.
With whispered wishes in the crackling fire,
And potatoes dancing, oh how they inspire!

Old boots debate the best of paths,
As marshmallow fellows giggle and laugh.
A chair with four legs starts to hum,
While a sleepy cat dreams of some crumb.

Every crackle brings a chuckle or two,
As the dog concocts a scheme anew.
Retreating from blizzards with a wink and a jig,
In this cozy den, life's a wild gig.

Let the outside world freeze and sway,
Here, shenanigans are at play.
With love and laughter, we always fit,
In this hearth of whispers, we endlessly sit.

Lullaby Under the Eaves

Beneath the shingles, cats do play,
Squirrels plotting for the snack buffet.
Tickles of laughter in the rain's soft dance,
Dreams chase the shadows, all at a glance.

Pillows like clouds, floating away,
I swear I saw a moose in the doorway!
Cuddles and chuckles echo the night,
A gathering of giggles until daylight.

The lamp flickers, dancing like a fool,
Jumped out of socks, 'cause socks can drool!
Chirping of crickets sings in delight,
As we crack jokes 'til the morning light.

Here's to the ruckus, a cozy retreat,
Where troubles get stuck in laughter's seat.
Wrapped in warmth and a blanket's embrace,
We nod off in joy, lost in this space.

Respite from the World

Here in the corner where chaos can't go,
Cabbage patch dolls lead a silent show.
Bubbles in cups, they float and they pop,
Time to unwind, let the giggles drop.

Flying tea kettles on invisible wings,
Whistling tunes of the silliest things!
Slippers like raccoons sneak across the floor,
A pastry parade through the wide-open door.

Under the table, the snacks start to flee,
Cookies in hiding, oh, living so free!
Between the cushions, there's treasure galore,
Laughter and wonder keep asking for more.

A refuge of whimsy where we dance and sing,
Life is a circus under this roofing.
So many sighs of relief in this space,
We'll wrap up our worries in a cozy embrace.

Arched Abode

Beneath the arch, we giggle and play,
Cartoons come alive, much to our dismay!
Jellybean bouquets scatter on the floor,
Candy-coated dreams ignite the rapport.

Puppies flip-flop in a furry parade,
Hats too big, on whose head are they made?
Laughter the wallpaper, bright as can be,
Chasing the blues till we're all back with glee.

Rain drumming gently, a rhythmic embrace,
Poking through puddles, oh what a race!
Here in our haven, the thunder can't scare,
For we've got umbrellas of joy everywhere.

Tucked under blankets, the world feels so grand,
With a sprinkle of giggles, together we stand.
In this archway of fun, so blissfully free,
We'll dance out our fears like they're made of confetti.

Sheltered by Hope

Against the rain, we huddle in cheer,
Clouds gather round, but we've got no fear.
Dancing with shadows that stretch and sway,
Biting back giggles that beg to play.

Muffins fly in from the oven with glee,
Who knew breakfast could be so fishy?
Wobbly whispers tumble down the hall,
Banana peels race as we all take a fall.

Under the beams, the sky can't inquire,
As we build a kingdom of dreams that inspire.
Fortress of laughter and whimsy galore,
Here's our escape from the world we abhor.

With every chuckle, our spirits will soar,
Finding the joy just outside of the door.
Wrapped in the giggles that promise a way,
We cherish these moments, come what may.

A Shield Against the Storm

When raindrops dance like they're in a band,
It's nice to be dry, with snacks close at hand.
The thunder may rumble, the lightning may flash,
But I'll be here munching, oh what a stash!

Fluffy pillows pile up to the sky,
As gusts of wind whirl, I'll just sit and sigh.
The weather may rage, but I'm snug like a bug,
In my cozy fortress, I'll just give a shrug.

The roof over my head, it's a glorious sight,
It keeps out the storms, and it feels so right.
With blankets and laughter, we'll laugh and we'll lean,
Who knew being lazy could feel like a dream?

So here's to the shelter, where giggles abound,
With memories made, and comfort profound.
When chaos erupts, I'll continue to stay,
With snacks and good vibes, come what may!

Nurtured by the Ceiling

Under the ceiling, life feels just grand,
When snacks are around, I've got plenty at hand.
With laughter that echoes, and chaos that swirls,
I'll dance in my PJs, a whirl of twirls!

As the rain taps a beat, I'll join in the fun,
A kitchen adventure? Oh, how it's begun!
From silly concoctions that bubble and pop,
To a feast for the senses—never will stop!

The ceiling protects from the world's wild grip,
Turning chaos to calm with each silly quip.
My pet is my partner, our bond cannot break,
Together we triumph, for fun's own sweet sake!

So here's to our haven, where giggles arise,
With snacks on the table and joy in our eyes.
In this playful palace, life's never too rough,
For we are all nurtured, with laughter enough!

Cloister of Solace

In a cloister adorned with cushions and quirks,
I find my retreat from the world's silly lurks.
Where giggles collide with the softest of sighs,
And a fortress of blankets, oh what a prize!

The cats think they rule this plush kingdom of dreams,
While I plot hearty laughter and sprightly schemes.
With popcorn in hand and a movie to play,
We'll shake off the boredom, come what may!

The walls hold the secrets of chuckles we've shared,
Through mishaps and blunders, they've truly declared:
Each moment a treasure, each joke has a spark,
And here in my cloister, my heart leaves its mark.

So lift up your voices and let the fun soar,
For in this vast domain, there's always room for more.
As shadows retreat and the sun dips below,
In this silly sanctuary, we'll let the joy flow!

Tranquil Asylum

In my tranquil asylum, where silliness rules,
With laughter as currency, I welcome the fools.
Pillows encircle like they're ready to fight,
Each giggly encounter turns wrong into right.

A dance in the kitchen, a spin on the floor,
As ingredients tumble, we're never a bore.
With chocolate on faces, and flour on toes,
The recipe calls for giggles, not woes!

The quiet of chaos, it makes my heart sing,
While if thumps on the roof bring the wildest of swings,
I'll tether my dreamland on whimsy alone,
For joy is the language, I've happily grown.

So here in my haven, may the fun never cease,
With dances and laughter, there's always a feast.
In this tranquil asylum, our spirits take flight,
As we giggle and play, till the fall of the night!

Asylum of Warmth

In a blanket fort, I reign supreme,
With snacks galore, it's quite the dream.
My loyal cats assess the scene,
Cozy kingdom, so serene.

Cushions stacked, a chair for thrones,
Here I declare, I'm never alone.
Scattered toys, my kingdom's loot,
In my fortress, life's a hoot!

A rogue sock slips, then we all giggle,
Fortress of fluff, my heart's a wiggle.
Let the world spin outside in strife,
In my lair, I find pure life!

Fortress built with laughs and cheer,
Diving in snacks without a fear.
Here I'll shelter like a pro,
In my hideout—come steal the show!

Serenity's Overhang

Under a desk, the chaos reigns,
Where grown-ups stumble, but I've got gains.
Painted skies and cartoon moons,
In my hideout, I hum sweet tunes.

A paperclip for a doorknob, yes!
I'll lock out worries, no need to stress.
With vibrant crayons and doodled dreams,
In my own world, I burst at the seams.

When lunch rolls by, it's quite a farce,
I feast on sugar, and then I dance!
Between the chaos, I'm feeling grand,
This chaotic haven is truly planned.

The snacks are sparse, but joy's not rare,
Under this desk, no need for care.
With giggles echoing, I sit in bliss,
Here in my nook, nothing's amiss!

Protection from the Tempest

When rain clouds shuffle and begin to pout,
I'll grab my umbrella, it's time for a shout!
Dancing in puddles, splashes galore,
Laughing off storms, what's life without more?

With rubber boots, I tackle the squish,
Each leap a joy, like a fish with a wish.
Neighbors peek out, they shake their heads,
To handle the rain, I dance instead!

I'll invite the wind for a jolly good sway,
With my sparkly jacket, I'll brighten the gray.
In the storm's embrace, I'm never alone,
I'll twirl through the thunder, a fun-loving drone!

Each crack of lightning, I do not flee,
I'm the maestro of my own jubilee.
Inside my heart, sunshine still beams,
Here in this tempest, I sail on dreams!

Portal to Peace

In a garden, I seek shelter from noise,
Among the daisies, I find my joys.
A squirrel rushes, stealing my snack,
But oh, the giggles, there's no looking back!

Beneath the branches, I make a camp,
With a cheeky grin, I'm quite the champ.
Butterflies flutter, an audience rare,
My private theater, filled with flair.

I pluck a flower, wear it like a crown,
My royal throne—it's flour-streaked brown.
With every tickle from the breeze's touch,
In nature's arms, I love it so much.

This safe retreat, where laughter sways,
With rhythms of nature, I dream away.
Here in my haven, the world fades afar,
The portal to peace, where I am the star!

Parapet of Reflection

Sitting up high, I sip my tea,
My cat plots schemes under the tree.
Reflecting on life, with just a grin,
Why buy the world when I can just spin?

The clouds hang low, a fluffy disguise,
Building castles, chasing pies.
With every sigh, the world takes flight,
How delightful to know I'm just right!

Neighbors below, they wave and shout,
As I dance around, there's joy, no doubt.
With laughter and crumbs, I claim my throne,
Who needs a crown when I have this bone?

From this high perch, all worries fade,
Life's silly moments nicely displayed.
So raise a toast from atop my space,
With humor and glee, I embrace my place!

Embracing the Elements

Rain drops fall like a rhythmic beat,
While I pirouette 'round my little seat.
The sun peeks through just to say hi,
As I slip on my socks and start to fly!

A gust of wind turns my hat on its head,
I chase butterflies while others dread.
With mud on my shoes and glee in my eyes,
I leap like a frog, oh, what a surprise!

Snowflakes flutter, a cold tickle's kiss,
I tumble and laugh—oh, life's full of bliss!
In cozy corners or stormy blight,
I twirl with the breeze, feeling just right.

Each element's twist brings laughter worth keeping,
With my heart in the clouds, dreams leaping and leaping.
So bring on the rain, let the tempests unfurl,
In my fantastic world, there's laughter to swirl!

Vaulted Embrace

Beneath the arches, I find my glee,
With echoes of laughter bouncing free.
Every beam above, whispers a tune,
I dance in the shadows; oh, what a boon!

The ceiling's a canvas for my grand dreams,
Painting the air with funny schemes.
I juggle the stars and hop with delight,
While my dog barks, claiming the night!

Chimney smoke dances, a whimsical waltz,
As I ponder my weirdest faults.
And if the moon giggles at my noise,
I shrug, for it's me who knows what joys!

With vaulted hugs that cradle my fears,
I toast with the moon, shedding old tears.
In this embrace of the comical kind,
I bask in the warmth, leaving worries behind!

Sanctuary from Strife

High above chaos, I claim my spot,
Where troubles dissolve and silliness is sought.
Every nuisance, a comical ploy,
In my fortress of fun, I find pure joy.

Giggles and chuckles fill the air,
When the world feels heavy, I just don't care.
My sanctuary, a laughter-lit room,
Swirling with quirk and dispelling all gloom.

A pillow for wisdom, a blanket for jest,
Within these confines, I find my best.
Ticklish moments and playful delights,
Laughter my sword, shining bright in the nights.

So here I will sit, in my cozy nest,
With sparkles of humor, life feels blessed.
In this haven from trials and tease,
I treasure each giggle, each moment of ease!

Enclosure of Ease

In a space where laughter rings,
And chaos takes a break,
The cushions bounce like happy things,
Embracing all mistakes.

Jelly beans and giggling fits,
We build a fort of fun,
With silly hats and random wits,
Our day has just begun.

When laundry piles begin to rise,
We wear them for a crown,
With sock puppets that mesmerize,
Let's not let smiles drown.

As toys invade our sacred ground,
And teddies start to dance,
In this joyful battleground,
There's laughter in every glance.

Vaulted Peace

Beneath the arch of childhood dreams,
A trampoline of cheer,
Where nothing's ever as it seems,
We float out on a leer.

The pizza rolls create a feast,
While soda streams abound,
We silence worries, not the least,
With giggles all around.

The walls may crinkle under weight,
As whispers turn to roars,
In this fortress, small and great,
It's joy that often soars.

Dancing cats and painted skies,
In our bubble, all is bright,
We laugh until we start to cry,
In our vaulted world of light.

Canopy of Kindness

Under branches, warm and wide,
A refuge made of care,
Where friendly hearts and smiles collide,
And burdens lift into the air.

With snacks and games and stories spun,
The fun is truly mad,
We race, we play, we chase the sun,
And never feel too bad.

The jellybeans will always stick,
Like memories we treasure,
In moments that just feel like magic,
We find our funniest pleasure.

As laughter cascades like a stream,
This canopy's our nest,
In a world that feels like a dream,
Where kindness knows no rest.

Nestled Above the Noise

In our hideaway from daily grind,
   Where silliness takes flight,
Each murmur turns to joy we find,
   In chuckles of delight.

The pillows act as laughter's throne,
   With giggles all around,
A secret lair we call our own,
   Where funny thoughts abound.

We toss the rules right out the door,
   And dance like no one's there,
   With pizza slices we adore,
   And antics free of care.

Each noise from life fades far away,
   In this realm of witty prose,
   We revel in our funny play,
Nestled safe, we're free to doze.

www.ingramcontent.com/pod-product-compliance
Lightning Source LLC
Chambersburg PA
CBHW060115230426
43661CB00003B/199